Different Like Me

Sherri Henderson

Illustrated by Ani Barmashi

Different Like Me
By Sherri Henderson

Copyright © 2018 by Sherri Henderson

First Edition

All rights reserved. No part of this publication may be reproduced, distributed, or transmitted in any form or by any means, including photocopying, recording, or other electronic methods, without the prior written permission of the publisher, except in the case of brief quotations embodied in critical reviews and certain other noncommercial uses permitted by copyright law.

For permission requests, write to the publisher.
Attention: Permissions Coordinator at the address below:

Henderson Haven, Inc.
772 Foxridge Center Dr.
Orange Park, FL 32065
www.HendersonHaven.org

ISBN: 978-1-7320118-2-3 (Print Edition)
ISBN: 978-1-7320118-3-0 (Ebook Edition)

Library of Congress Control Number: 2018913586

Ordering information:
Quantity sales. Special discounts are available on quantity purchases by corporations, associations, and others. For details, contact the publisher at the address above.

Printed in the United States of America

Thank you to my husband, Lee, for making this book a reality and for always believing in me. Thanks also to all those kids in my life who challenge me daily to think outside the box and be creative – Trey, Cameron, Marla, Michelle, Grace, and all those other kids whose lives I've been privileged to be a small part of. And, Trey, this book exists because you asked me, "Why did God make me different?" Love you all!

Some of us are kind of short while others are super tall.

Some of our hands are really BIG and some of them are small.

Some of our music's loud and hard, we love our rock and roll.

But some of us just love the music that simply soothes our soul.

Some of us can run and play while some of us just sit.

Some of us may always win and some will never quit.

Did you find the butterfly in every illustration?

Why the butterfly?

We use the butterfly for our logos because of "The Butterfly Effect." The meaning comes from a 1972 talk given by Edward Lorenz to the American Association for the Advancement of Science describing the chaos theory titled, "Does The Flap Of A Butterfly's Wings In Brazil Set Off A Tornado in Texas." In other words, the ripples of a very small change can make a huge difference down the road.

Founded in 2003 by Lee and Sherri Henderson, Henderson Haven, Inc's. non-profit services continue to help ensure a self-determined life and community inclusion for all. Presuming competence in everyone, the staff of Henderson Haven assist those they serve reach their full potential. With services ranging from pre-school, private school, transition, to community supports, Henderson Haven continues to assist everyone in living the lives we all take for granted.

For more information or to donate:
www.HendersonHaven.org

 **Sherri Henderson** founded Henderson Haven, Inc. with her husband, Lee, when families began seeking her advice on providing their children with the same opportunities her son with Down Syndrome, Trey, has had in his life. Always believing that any individual has the capacity to live on their terms regardless of their perceived abilities, she has always fought both personally and professionally to help ensure those rights for all.

 **Ani Barmashi** lives in Tirana, Albania where she studied architecture for 5 years at Polytechnic University. Having a love of drawing and illustrating all her life, she now operates her own studio specializing in architectural drawing but also works in book, magazine and website illustration.

This is Ani's second collaboration with Sherri and she looks forward to others in the future.

Ani can be reached at anibarmashi@gmail.com

www.ingramcontent.com/pod-product-compliance
Lightning Source LLC
Chambersburg PA
CBRC092058200426
43209CB00067B/1867